Track Diagrams – Scotland and Is

These diagrams include the lines of British Rail's former Scottish Region, t railways and industrial layouts. It is, in general, up-to-date to 1st Januar

The first edition, for Scotland only, appeared in 1987 and there have been many changes since then. This new edition has been completely redrawn to a larger scale and now shows full details of yards, as well as numerous other improvements, including the addition of an index.

Mileages often vary slightly between different official records, but, in general, those given in the latest Sectional Appendix have been used. Station mileages are usually taken from the mid-point of the platforms, or, in the case of a terminus, the buffer stops.

These diagrams have been compiled substantially from information supplied from various British Rail Sources, supplemented by other data and amended from observations. In some cases distinctions between BR ownership and other parties are not shown and no inferences concerning ownership should therefore be drawn.

The assistance of numerous BR officials is gratefully acknowledged. Other acknowledgements are due to Branch Line Society/Rodger Wilkinson, Michael Oakley, Brian Philp, Simon Lowe, Wreford Voge, Ian Scotchman, Eric Rudkin, John Stratton and, for the Isle of Man, Graham Warhurst, Operations Superintendent, Isle of Man Railways, R.P. Hendry and A. Beard, Groudle Glen Railway. Also representatives of the other private and preserved systems featured.

Cartographer: John Yonge   Consultant editor: Gerald Jacobs

KEY

———	Running line	93	Whole mileposts, shown on the appropriate side of the line
———	Siding *A broken line indicates 'in situ' but out of use, proposed or under construction.*	■	Platform with number
		⊏⊐	Provisional proposed platform
		▢	Platform out of use
Former BR regional boundary		⊠(P)	Signal box with code
Signal box/centre area limits		⊠	Gate box
Perth (P) SB | Edinburgh (E) SC		▫	Ground frame
⊣– –⊢ Tunnel		⊗	Radio Electronic Block Post
Viaduct		o	Water Tower
Level crossing (signalled)		∧	Summit
Crossing (telephone)		•	Location spot
Track signalled in both directions (a double arrow indicates normal direction of travel)		86.34	Distance in miles and chains (80 chains to 1 mile; 22 yards – about 20 metres – equal 1 chain)
Private siding boundary, often marked by a gate		ECM	ELR (Engineers Line Reference)
Wall			

PRICE £5.00   ISBN: 0 900609 95 8

Published by the Quail Map Company, 31 Lincoln Road, Exeter EX4 2DZ (Telephone Exeter 430277) and printed by the Brightsea Press Ltd, Exeter.
© John Yonge, Gerald Jacobs and The Quail Map Company. February 1993.

ABBREVIATIONS

ABCL	Automatic Barrier Crossing – (Locally monitored)
ABP	Associated British Ports
AHB	Automatic Half Barriers
AOCL	Automatic Open Crossing (Locally monitored by train crew)
AOCR	Automatic Open Crossing (Remotely monitored)
ARR	Arrival
BC	British Coal
bdy	boundary
BCH	Branch
BR	British Rail
Cal	Former Caledonian Railway
CCTV	Closed circuit television
CE	Civil Engineer
COM	Change of mileage
CR	Cripple siding
CW	Carriage washer
C & W	Carriage & Wagon
DCE	Down Civil Engineers Line
DEP	Departure
DGL	Down Goods Loop
DN	Down
DPL	Down Passenger Loop
DRS	Down Refuge Siding
E	East
e	electrified
EGF	Emergency Ground Frame
EMU	Electric multiple-unit
ER	Former Eastern Region
FP	Fuelling point
GB & K Jt	former Glasgow, Barrhead & Kilmarnock Joint Railway
GDS	Goods
GF	Ground Frame
GL	Goods loop
GN of S	Former Great North of Scotland Railway
GS	Goods Shed
GSP	Ground Switch Panel
GSW	former Glasgow & South Western Railway
H	Headshunt
HH	Hopper House
High	former Highland Railway
HST	High Speed Train
Jn	Junction
Jt	Joint
LC	Level Crossing
LHS	Loco. Holding Siding
LMR	former London Midland Region
LMS	former London, Midland & Scottish Railway (1923-47)
LNE	former London & North Eastern Railway (1923-47)

LNW	former London & North Western Railway
LPG	Liquid petroleum gas
LS	Locomotive shed
LW	Locomotive washer
M & EE	Mechanical & Electrical Engineer
ME	Maintenance Engineer
MGR	Merry-go-round
MOD	Ministry of Defence
N	North
n	Not electrified
NB	former North British Railway
NE	former North Eastern Railway
NIRU	Not in regular use
OHC	Overhead crane
OOU	Out of use
Open	Open crossing – no lights
OTM	On-track Maintenance
P	Points padlocked
PS	Private siding
PSB	Power signal box
PW	Permanent Way
RAF	Royal Air Force
RC	Remotely controlled barriers
REC	Reception
RETB	Radio Electronic Token Block
R/G	Miniature red/green warning lights
RNAD	Royal Naval Armaments Depot
RR	Run-round
S	South
SB	Signal box
SC	Signalling Centre
ScR	former Scottish Region
Sdg(s)	Siding(s)
SD	Sand Drag
SF	Shunting Frame
SN	Shunt neck
SS	Shunt spur
S & TE	Signal & Telegraph Engineer
TL	Traffic lights
TMD	Traction Maintenance Depot
TMO	Trainmen operated
T & RS	Traction & Rolling Stock
UF	Up Fast
UGL	Up Goods Loop
UKAEA	United Kingdom Atomic Energy Authority
UPL	Up Passenger loop
URS	Up Refuge Siding
UT	Up Through
W	West
WB	Weighbridge
X	(After level crossing type abbreviations) – the crossing works automatically for movements in the wrong direction
yds	yards

In the same series:
2. England, East and Anglia *(out of print, new edition, late 1993?)*
3. Western Region £5.00
4. London Midland Region £6.95
5. England, South & London Underground *(we regret the long delay, which is beyond our control, but hope to publish later in 1993)*
The Quail Map Company produces and imports railway maps of various countries and cities. A catalogue will be sent on request.

INDEX FOR SCOTLAND

ABERDEEN	17A	BURNSIDE	7	DUIRINISH	22D
ABERDOUR	13	BURNTISLAND	13	DUKE STREET	7
Abington	10B	BUSBY	7	DUMBARTON CENTRAL	6B
ACHANALT	22F			DUMBARTON EAST	6B
ACHNASHEEN	22E	Cadder	7	DUNBAR	11B
ACHNASHELLACH	22E	CALEDONIAN RLY (BRECHIN) LTD	16Ba	DUNCRAIG	22D
ADDIEWELL	10D	Cambus Junction	15A	DUNDEE	16B
AIRBLES	8	CAMBUSLANG	7	DUNFERMLINE	13
AIRDRIE	8	Camperdown	16B	DUNKELD & BIRNAM	19A
ALEXANDRA PARADE	7	CARDENDEN	13	DUNLOP	4
ALEXANDRIA	6B	CARDONALD	5A	Dunragit	2A
Alford Valley Railway	17B	CARDROSS	6B	DUNROBIN CASTLE	20B
ALNESS	18D	CARFIN	8	Dunrod	5B
ALTNABREAC	20D	CARLISLE	1A		
Alves Junction	18A	CARLUKE	10E	EAST KILBRIDE	7
ANDERSTON	7	Carmont	16D	EASTERHOUSE	8
ANNAN	1C	CARMYLE	8	Eastfield	7
Annat	22A	CARNTYNE	7	Eastriggs	1C
ANNIESLAND	7	CARSTAIRS	10E	Edinburgh Airport	12
ARBROATH	16C	CARNOUSTIE	16B	EDINBURGH WAVERLEY	11A
Ardeer	4	CARRBRIDGE	19D	ELGIN	18A
ARDGAY	20A	CARTSDYKE	5B	ERROL	16A
ARDLUI	21A	CATHCART	7	Evanton	18D
ARDROSSAN HARBOUR	4	CESSNOCK	9B	EXHIBITION CENTRE	7
ARDROSSAN SOUTH BEACH	4	Chalmerston	2C		
ARDROSSAN TOWN	4	CHARING CROSS	7	FAIRLIE	4
ARGYLE STREET	7	Charlestown	15A	FALKIRK GRAHAMSTON	9A
ARISAIG	22B	CLARKSTON	7	FALKIRK HIGH	9A
ARROCHAR & TARBET	21A	CLELAND	8	FALKLAND YARD	3
ATTADALE	22E	Clunes	18C	FALLS OF CRUACHAN	21C
Auchincruive	3	CLYDEBANK	6A	FAULDHOUSE	10D
AUCHINDACHY	17E	CLYDEPORT	5B	FEARN	18D
AUCHINLECK	3	COATBRIDGE CENTRAL	8	Ferryhill Sidings	17A
AUCHMUTY	13	COATBRIDGE SUNNYSIDE	8	FORRES	18A
Auchterarder	16C	COATDYKE	8	FORSINARD	20D
AVIEMORE	19D	COCKENZIE	11A	FORT MATILDA	5B
AYR	3	COLTNESS	8	FORT WILLIAM	22A
		CONNEL FERRY	21C		
Baileyfield	11A	CORKERHILL	5A	GARELOCHHEAD	21A
BAILLIESTON	8	CORPACH	22A	GARROWHILL	8
BALLOCH	6B	CORROUR	21E	GARSCADDEN	6A
BALMOSSIE	16B	COWCADDENS	9B	Gartcosh	9A
BANAVIE	22A	COWDENBEATH	13	Gartshore	9A
BARASSIE	3	Cowlairs	7	GARVE	22F
BARGEDDIE	8	CRAIGENDORAN	6B	GEORGEMAS JUNCTION	20F
Barleith	3	Craigentinny	11A	GIFFEN	4
BARNHILL	7	Craiginches Yard	17A	GIFFNOCK	7
BARRHEAD	4,7	CRAIGLOCKHART	11A	GIRVAN	2B
BARRHILL	2B	CRAIGNURE	21Ba	GLASGOW CENTRAL	7
BARRY LINKS	16B	CRIANLARICH	21B	GLASGOW QUEEN STREET	7
BATHGATE	12	CROFTFOOT	7	GLASGOW UNDERGROUND	9B
BEARSDEN	7	Crombie	15A	GLENCARRAN	22E
BEASDALE	22B	CROOKSTON	5A	Glen Douglas	21A
BEATTOCK	10A,10B	CROSSHILL	7	GLENEAGLES	15B
BELLGROVE	7	CROSSMYLOOF	7	GLENFINNAN	22B
BELLSHILL	8	CROY	9A	GLENGARNOCK	4
BENBANE	2C	CULLODEN	19E	GLENROTHES with THORTON	13
BERWICK UPON TWEED	11C	CULRAIN	20A	Glenwilly	2A
BILSTON GLEN	11A	CUMBERNAULD	9A	GOLF STREET	16B
BIRKHILL	12	CUPAR	14C	GOLSPIE	20B
BISHOPBRIGGS	7	CURRIEHILL	10C	Gortan (Tayside)	21D
BISHOPTON	5A			GOUROCK	5B
Blackford	15B	Dalcross	18B	GOVAN	9B
BLACKFORD HILL	11A	DALMALLY	21C	GRANGEMOUTH	12
BLAIR ATHOLL	19B	DALMARNOCK	7	GRANTOWN-ON-SPEY	19D
BLAIRHILL	8	DALMENY	12	Grantshouse	11C
BLANTYRE	8	DALMUIR	6A	GREENFAULDS	9A
BOAT OF GARTEN	19D	DALNASPIDAL	19B	Greenhill Junctions	9A
BOGSTON	5B	DALREOCH	6B	Greenloaning	15B
BO'NESS	12	DALRY	4	GREENOCK CENTRAL	5B
BOWLING	6A	Dalrymple In	2C	GREENOCK WEST	5B
BRANCHTON	5B	DALWHINNIE	19C	Gretna Junction	1B
BRECHIN	16Ba	DEANSIDE	5A	GUNNIE	8
BREICH	10D	DINGWALL	18C,22F	Gushetfaulds	7
BRIDGE OF DUN	16Ba	DREM	11B		
BRIDGE OF ORCHY	21D	DRUMBRECK	7	HAIRMYRES	7
BRIDGE STREET	9B	Drongan	3	HAMILTON CENTRAL	8
BRIDGETON	7	DRUMCHAPEL	6A	HAMILTON WEST	8
BROOMLOAN	9B	DRUMGELLOCH	8	HARTWOOD	8
BRORA	20B	DRUMMUIR	17E	Hawkhead	5A
BROUGHTY FERRY	16B	DRUMRY	6A	HAYMARKET	11A
BUCHANAN STREET	9B	DUDDINGSTON	11A	HELENSBURGH CENTRAL	6B
BURGHEAD	18A	DUFFTOWN	17E	HELENSBURGH UPPER	6B

HELMSDALE	20C	LOCHGELLY	13
HIGH STREET	7	LOCHLUICHART	22F
HILLFOOT	7	LOCHWINNOCH	4
HILLHEAD	9B	LOCKERBIE	10A
Hillhouse Quarry	3	LONGANNET	15A
HILLINGTON EAST	5A	LONGNIDDRY	11B
HILLINGTON WEST	5A	LYNEDOCH	5B
Hillside	16D		
Hilton Junction	14C,16C	MALLAIG	22C
HOLYTOWN	8	Manuel	12
HUNTERSTON	4	MARKINCH	13
HUNTLY	17D	Maryhill	7
HYNDLAND	7	MAXWELL PARK	7
		MAYBOLE	2C
IBM	5B	Meadowhead	3
IBROX	9B	MENSTRIE	15A
INSCH	17C	METHIL	14B
Inveralmond	15D	Midcalder Junction	10D, 10E
INVERGORDON	18D	MILLERHILL YARD	11A
INVERGOWRIE	16A	MILLIKEN PARK	5A
INVERKEITHING	12,13	MILNGAVIE	7
INVERKIP	5B	MISK	4
INVERNESS	18B	MONIFIETH	16B
INVERURIE	17C	MONTROSE	16C
INVERSHIN	20A	MORAR	22C
IRVINE	4	MORNINGSIDE ROAD	11A
		MOSSPARK	5A
JOHNSTONE	5A	MOSSEND YARD	8
JORDANHILL	7	MOTHERWELL	8
		MOUNT FLORIDA	7
Kaimes	10E	MOUNT VERNON	8
KEITH	17D	Moy	19E
KEITH TOWN	17E	MUIR OF ORD	18C
KELVIN HALL	9B	MUIREND	7
KELVIN BRIDGE	9B	Mull and West Highland Rly	21Ba
Kennethmont	17C	MUSSELBURGH	11A
KENNISHEAD	7		
Kerr's Miniature Railway	16C	NAIRN	18B
KILDONAN	20C	NEILSTON	7
Kilkerran	2B	NEW CUMNOCK	2E
KILLOCH	3	Newbridge Junction	12
KILMARNOCK	3	NEWINGTON	11A
KILMAURS	4	NEWTON	7, 8
KILPATRICK	6A	NEWTONMORE	19C
KILWINNING	4	NEWTON-ON-AYR	3
KINBRACE	20C	Niddrie	11A
KINCARDINE	14A	NITSHILL	7
KINCRAIG	19C	NORTH BERWICK	11B
KINGHORN	13	NORTH QUEENSFERRY	12
KINGMOOR	1A		
KING'S PARK	7	OBAN	21C
KINGSKNOWE	10C	Oxwellmains	11C
KINGUSSIE	19C		
KINNEIL HALT	12	PAISLEY CANAL	5A
KINNING PARK	9B	PAISLEY GILMOUR ST.	5A
KIRKCALDY	13	PAISLEY ST. JAMES	5A
KIRKCONNEL	2E	PARTICK	7, 9B
KIRKHILL	7	PATTERTON	7
KIRKNEWTON	10E	PERTH	15D, 16A
KIRKWOOD	8	PITLOCHRY	19B
Kittybrewster	17B	Plean Junction	15A
KNOCKSHINNOCH	2E	PLOCKTON	22D
KYLE OF LOCHALSH	22D	POLLOKSHAWS EAST	7
		POLLOKSHAWS WEST	7
LADYBANK	14C	POLLOKSHIELDS EAST	7
LAIRG	20A	POLLOKSHIELDS WEST	7
LANARK	10E	Polmadie	7
LANGBANK	5A	Polmaise	15A
LANGSIDE	7	POLMONT	12
LARBERT	9A, 15A	Port Elphinstone	17C
LARGS	4	PORT GLASGOW	5B
Larkfield	7	PORTLETHEN	17A
Laurencekirk	16D	Portobello	11A
Law	8	Powderhall	11A
LEITH	11A	PRESTONPANS	11A
LENZIE	7, 9A	PRESTWICK	3
LEUCHARS	14C	PRIESTHILL & DARNLEY	7
LINLITHGOW	12		
LIVINGSTON NORTH	12	QUEEN'S PARK	7
LIVINGSTON SOUTH	10D		
Lochaber	22A	RANNOCH	21D
LOCHAILORT	22B	RAVENSCRAIG	8
LOCH AWE	21C	RENTON	6B
LOCH EIL OUTWARD BOUND	22A	Reston	11C
LOCHEILSIDE	22A	RICCARTON	3

ROGART	20B
Roseisle	18A
ROSYTH	13
ROSYTH NAVAL DOCKYARD	12
ROTHESAY DOCK	6A
Roughcastle Sdg	9A
ROY BRIDGE	21E
RUTHERGLEN	7
ST. ENOCH	9B
St. Fort	14D
ST. GEORGE'S CROSS	9B
ST. ROLLOX	7
SALTCOATS	4
SCOTSCALDER	20D
SCOTSTOUNHILL	6A
SHAWLANDS	7
SHETTLESTON	8
Shieldhall	5A
SHIELDMUIR	8
Shields	7
SHIELDS ROAD	9B
SHOTTS	8
SINGER	6A
SLATEFORD	10C, 11A
Slochd	19D
Smithy Lye	7
SOUTH GYLE	12
SPEAN BRIDGE	21E
SPRINGBURN	7
SPRINGFIELD	14C
Stanley Junction	19A
STEPPS	9A
STEVENSTON	4
STEWARTON	4
STIRLING	15A
STONEHAVEN	18A
STRANRAER HARBOUR	2A
Stranraer Town	2A
STRATHCARRON	22E
STRATHISLA	17A
STRATHSPEY RAILWAY	19D
STROMEFERRY	22D
TAIN	18D
Tarmstedt	21Ba
Tay Bridge	14D
TAYNUILT	21C
THORNLIEHEAD	7
THORNTON YARD	13
THORNTONHALL	7
THURSO	20F
Tomatin	19D
Torness	11C
TOROSAY	21Ba
TROON	3
TULLOCH	21E
Turkey Yard	7
TYNDRUM LOWER	21B
TYNDRUM UPPER	21B
UDDINGSTON	8
UPHALL	12
USAN	16C
WATERLOO	17B
WAVERLEY	11A
WEMYSS BAY	5B
WEST CALDER	10D
WEST KILBRIDE	4
WEST STREET	9B
WESTER HAILES	10C
WESTERTON	6A, 7
WESTFIELD	13
WHIFFLET	8
WHINHILL	5B
WHITECRAIGS	7
WICK	20F
WILLIAMWOOD	7
Winchburgh Jn	12
Windygates	14B
WISHAW	8
WOODHALL	5B
YOKER	6A

THURSO

20E

Georgemas
Junction

WICK

20D

20C

Helmsdale

20B

20A

18D

Invergordon

Burghead

Elgin

Keith

22F

DINGWALL

18C

18B

18A

17F

Dufftown

17E

17D

INVERNESS

22E

19E

17C

17B

22D

KYLE OF LOCHALSH

19D

Grantown-on-Spey

19D Strathspey Rly

Alford Valley Rly

17B

Waterloo
ABERDEEN

SKYE

Aviemore

17A

MALLAIG

19C

Stonehaven

22C

16D

22A

21E

FORT WILLIAM

19B

Caledonian Rly
Brechin

Montrose

16 Ba

Bridge of Dun

16C

21D

19A

MULL

21Ba

Craignure
Torosay

21C

21B

DUNDEE

16B

Arbroath

Mull & West
Highland Rly

OBAN

Crianlarich

16A

14D

15D PERTH

14C

21A

15B

15C

14C

Auchmuty
Thornton
13

Ladybank

15A

Westfield

Methil
14B

STIRLING

Alloa

Dunfermline

Kirkcaldy

15A

14A

13

Kin.

Balloch

6B 6B

G'mouth

12

Inverkeithing

North Berwick

Helensburgh

Milngavie

9A

GLASGOW

FALKIRK

Teith

EDINBURGH

11B

6A 7

9A

12

Gourock

7

Cumbernauld

12

Drem

Dunbar

5B

8

Bathgate

10C

11A

Millerhill

Wemyss Bay

Paisley

5A

8

Drumgelloch

Bilston Glen

Largs

5A

7

E.

8

10D

11C

BERWICK UPON TWEED

4

Neilston

Kilbride

Motherwell

10E

Hunterston

8

Newcastle
York
London

4

4

10E

Ardrossan

Lanark

Carstairs

ARRAN

3

Kilmarnock

10B

Troon

Barassie

3

3

AYR

3

Killoch

2C

Benbane

2E

10A

Girvan

2B

2D

Maxwelltown

Dumfries

1C

STRANRAER

2A

1B

1A

CARLISLE

Preston
Crewe
London

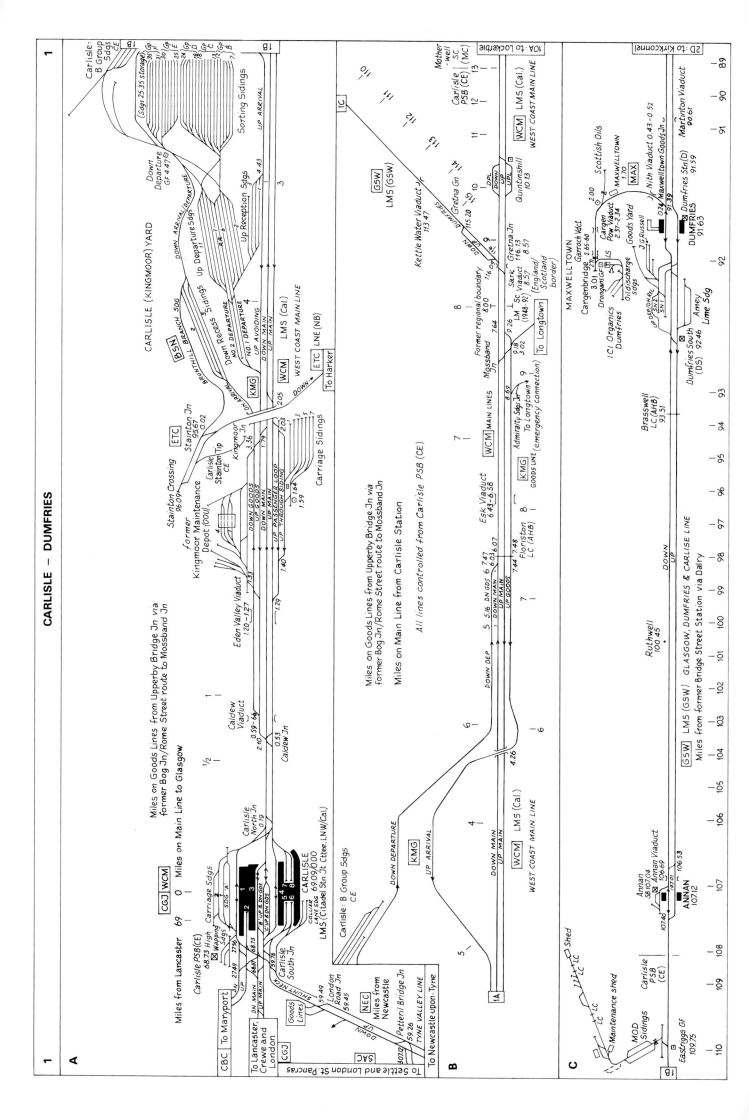

CARLISLE – DUMFRIES

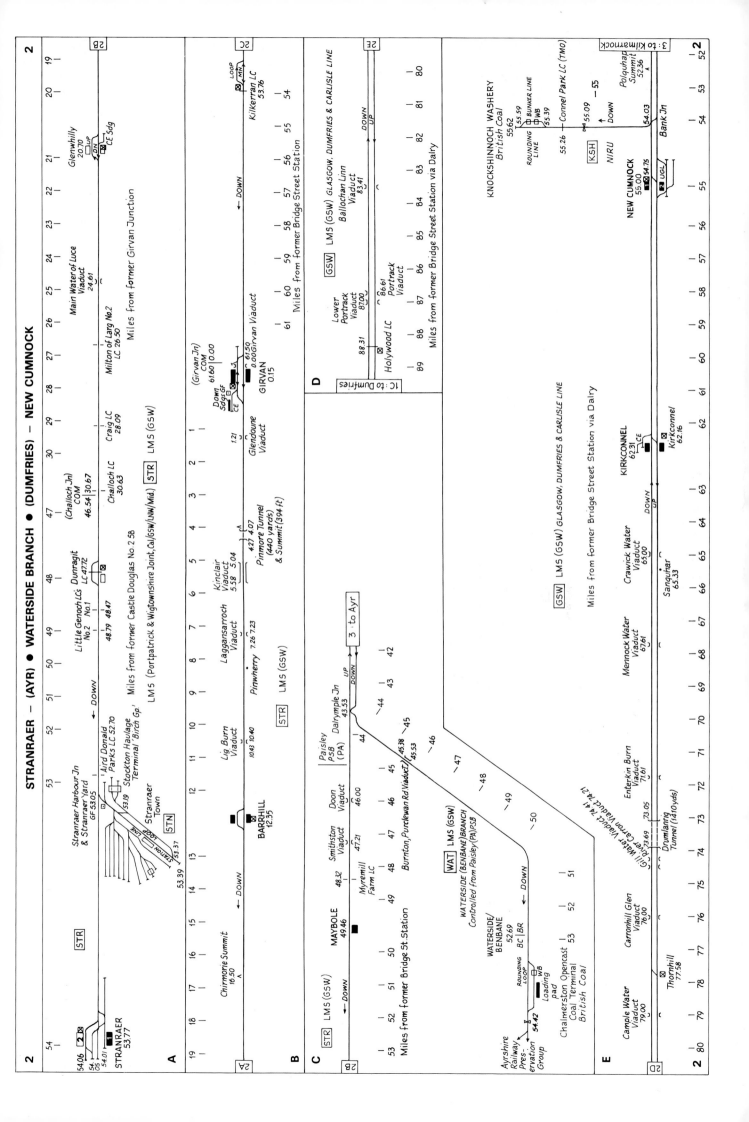

STRANRAER – (AYR) ● WATERSIDE BRANCH ● (DUMFRIES) – NEW CUMNOCK

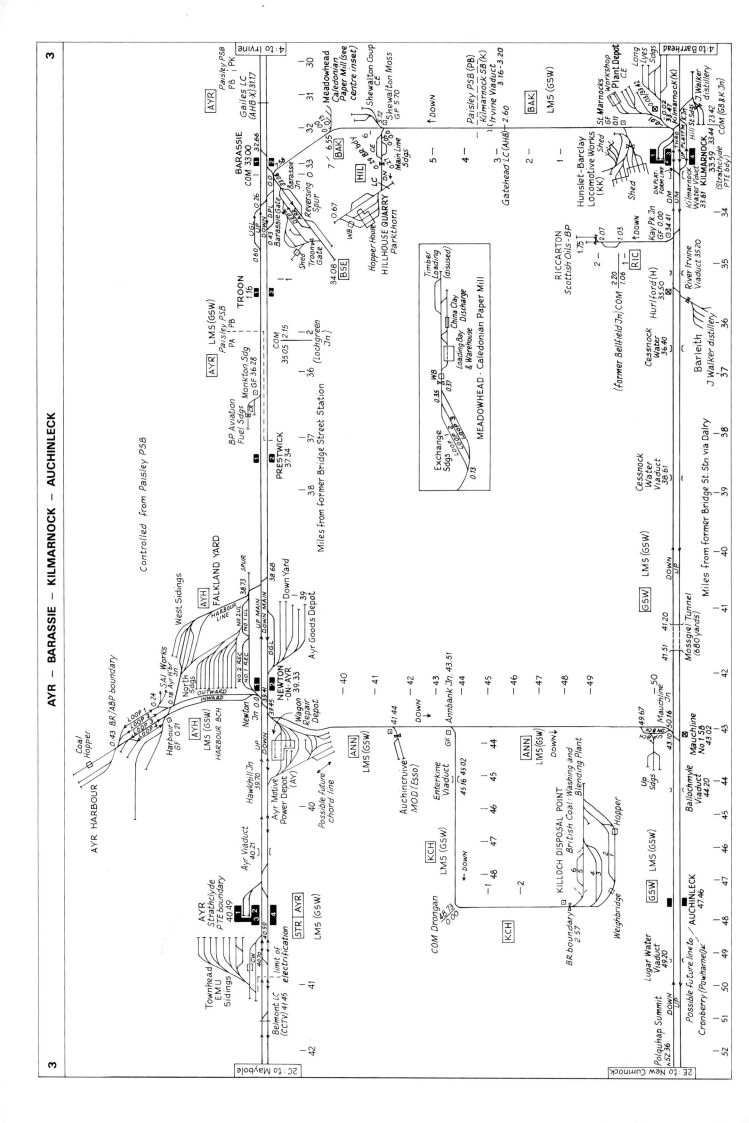

AYR – BARASSIE – KILMARNOCK – AUCHINLECK

IRVINE & LARGS – LOCHWINNOCH ● KILMAURS – BARRHEAD ● GIFFEN BRANCH

LARGS 42.07
Strathclyde PTE boundary
42

Admiralty Siding (Fairlie Pier)
Scottish Admiralty Nuclear Siding
GF 39.59
39.12
41

LGS | LMS (GSW)

Fairlie Tunnel 3057 (990 yards)
FAIRLIE 39.01
Fairlie High GF 38.72
40
39

Miles from former Bridge Street Station

HUNTERSTON
BS ore reduction plant
Low Level Sidings
LOCO RELEASE 3.07 2.71
Hunterston Causeway LC (AOCL) 262
–2
–1
CR
HUN
NIRU

not electrified

Ore bunker ORE SDG
LOCO RELEASE
Coal bunker (Loading Tower)
WB Coal SDG (NIRU)
SP CR
WB
0.07 0.36 0.51
BR limit
0.00 0.03
36.43 36.47
Hunterston Jn
HUNTERSTON Ore Terminal (High Level)
1,2 - ORE DEP
3 - ARRIVAL
4 - COAL DEP
SP - SPARE SDG
38
37

ARDROSSAN HARBOUR 31.35
31.38 Strathclyde PTE boundary
Ardrossan Harbour LC (CCTV) 31.07
Paisley PSB PK | PH
WEST KILBRIDE 35.10
LGS | LMS (GSW)
ARH
ARDROSSAN TOWN 31.00
Princes Street LC (CCTV) 31.07
30.44
36
35

All lines controlled from Paisley PSB

Paisley PSB PG | PE
AYR | LMS (GSW)
UP AYR
DOWN AYR
LOCHWINNOCH 15.57
Lochwinnoch Crossovers 15.24
19 18 17 16 15 14 13

Young Transport (closed)
UGL
GLENGARNOCK 19.63
19.74 19.58 19.37
CE
20

Miles from former Bridge Street Station

Paisley PSB PK | PG
AYR | LMS (GSW)
UP AYR
DOWN AYR
DALRY 22.42
23 24 25

Roche Products
Workshop
Inwards Outwards
HH WB
Swinlees Sdg
UPL GF 21.38
DPL
UP AYR 20.78
DOWN AYR
BROWNHILL CE 506
Brownhill CE GF 21.07
21.28
21.74
21 22

Miles from former Gorbals Junction

(Barrmill Jn)
0.19
1350 Lugton
0.00
UP DN LOOP
Wm. Clegg contractors
Lugton Water Viaduct 0.68-0.70
14

COM (Kilbirnie Jn)
0.00
2.70
COM (Giffen Jn)
0.00
Glazert Viaduct 16.00
DUNLOP 16.02
GIF | LMS (GSW)
16 17

GIFFEN RNAD
0.23

Stewartol Viaduct (Annick Water Viaduct) 18.41
STEWARTON 18.20
18 19

ARDROSSAN SOUTH BEACH 30.38
30.38
EMU sdg
Holm Jn
Limit of electrification
3.00
SALTCOATS 29.55
Stevenston LC (CCTV) 28.31
STEVENSTON 28.25
LGS | LMS (GSW)
DGL
27.75 27.69
0.00/28.14
–30 –29 –28 27

Gourock Burn Viaduct 33.07
UP & DN LARGS
UP FREIGHT
32 33 34
31

MISK | NIRU
0.57
MISK
ICI Petro Chemicals
Ardeer ICI Organics
Nylon works
NIRU NIRU NIRU
ICI Snodgrass Nobel Explosives
STG 0.28
0.00
27.76
Bogside
Longford Viaduct 27.00
Byrehill Jn
26.75
26.76
BYL
NM 0.00
0.00
UP LARGS
DOWN LARGS
DRS
NIRU
20 21 26.79

Dubbs Jn 26.69
26
KILWINNING 26.00
26.08 26.08
25.71 Kilwinning Jn
DRS CE UGL CE
27

AYR | LMS (GB&K Joint) (Cal & GSW)
UP AYR
DOWN AYR

KILMAURS 21.50
Carmel Viaduct 22.00
22

Long Lyes Sdgs
Mineral Sdgs
1 OOU
Blue Circle Cement (NIRU)
CE
Irvine Yard & Depot
IRVINE 29.28
29.40 29.34
Irvine Freight Depot
IRE
5.35 NIRU
CE
Irvine Jn 5.51
5.25 miles from Kilmarnock via Dreghorn
28 29 30 23

GBK | LMS (GB&K Joint) (Cal & GSW)

5: to Paisley
7: to Glasgow
3: to Kilmarnock
3: to Barassie & Ayr

BARRHEAD 6.77
Gateside Viaduct 7.61
BAY PLATFM
(8D) 6.70
UM DM SD
7 8

GBK | LMS (GB&K Joint) (Cal & GSW)

DOWN

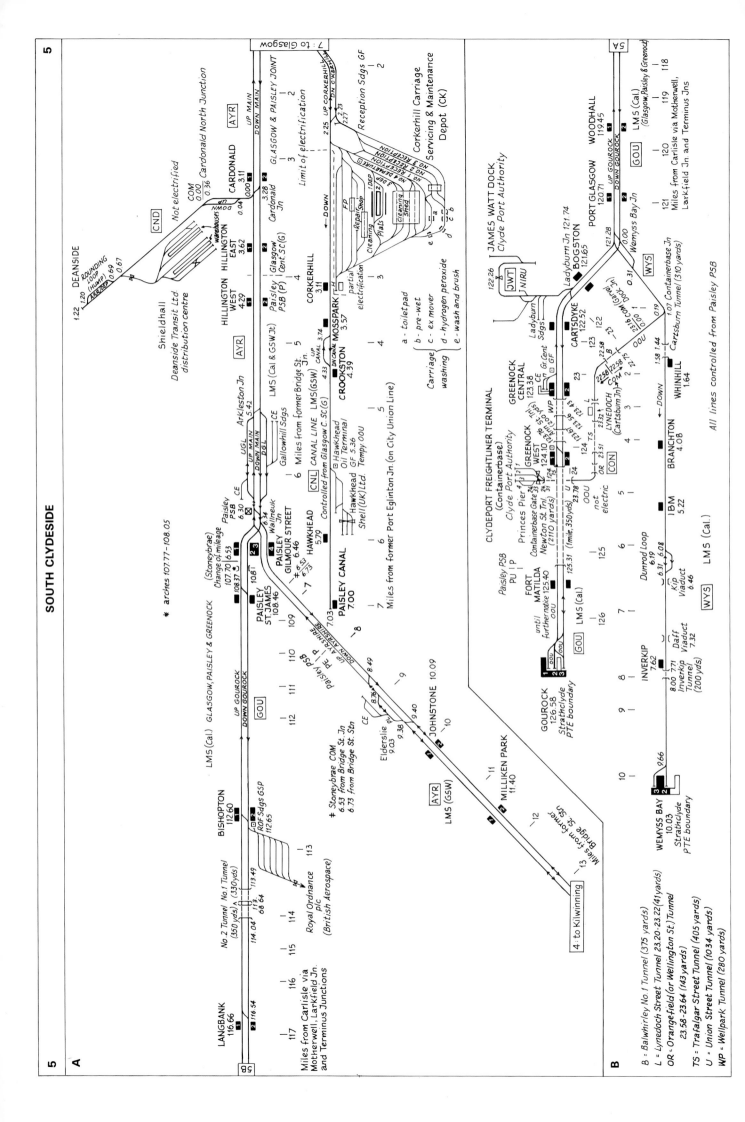

SOUTH CLYDESIDE

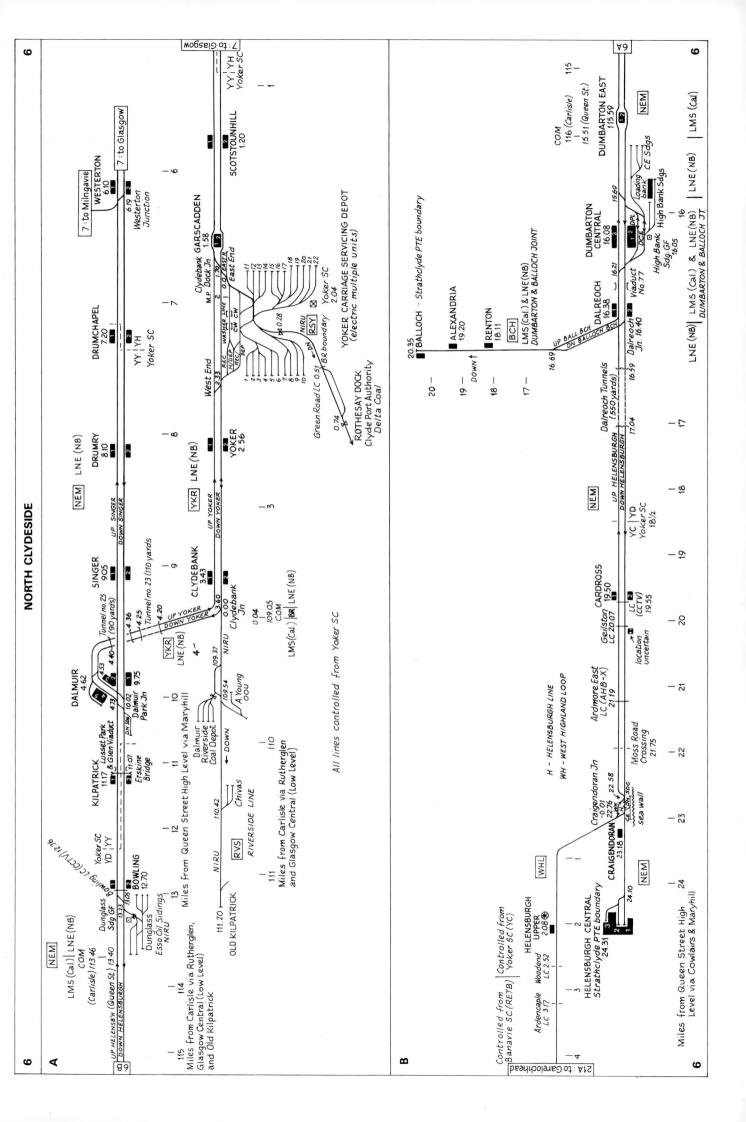

NORTH CLYDESIDE

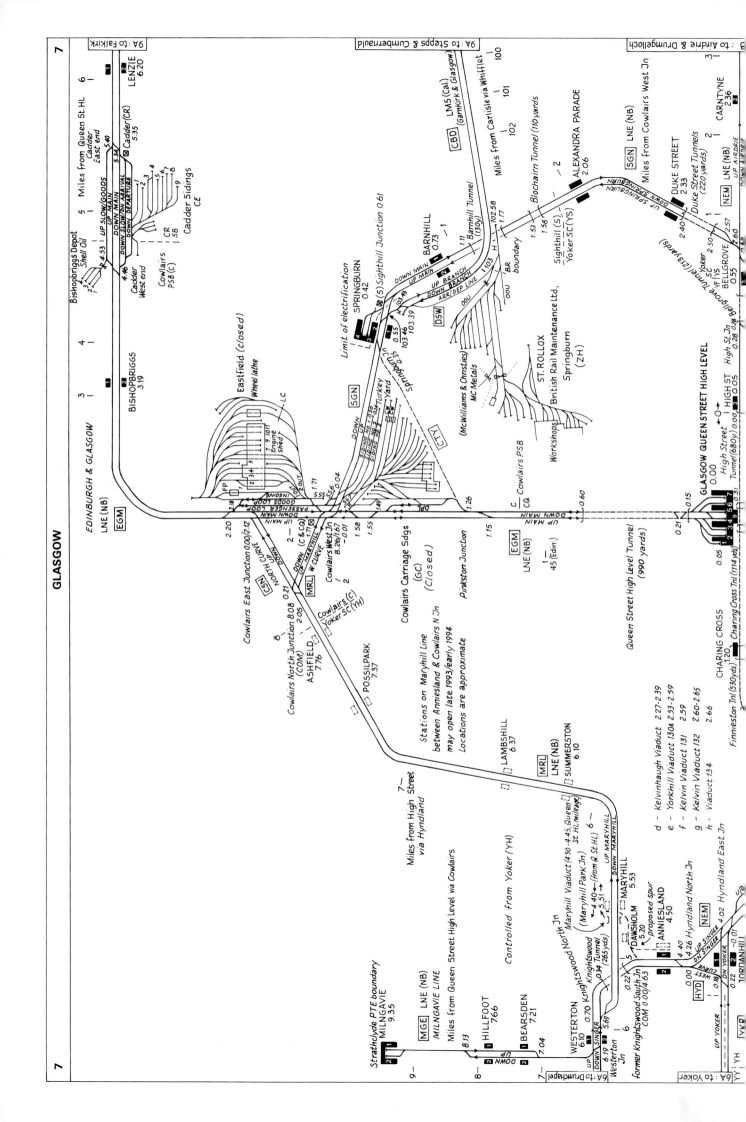

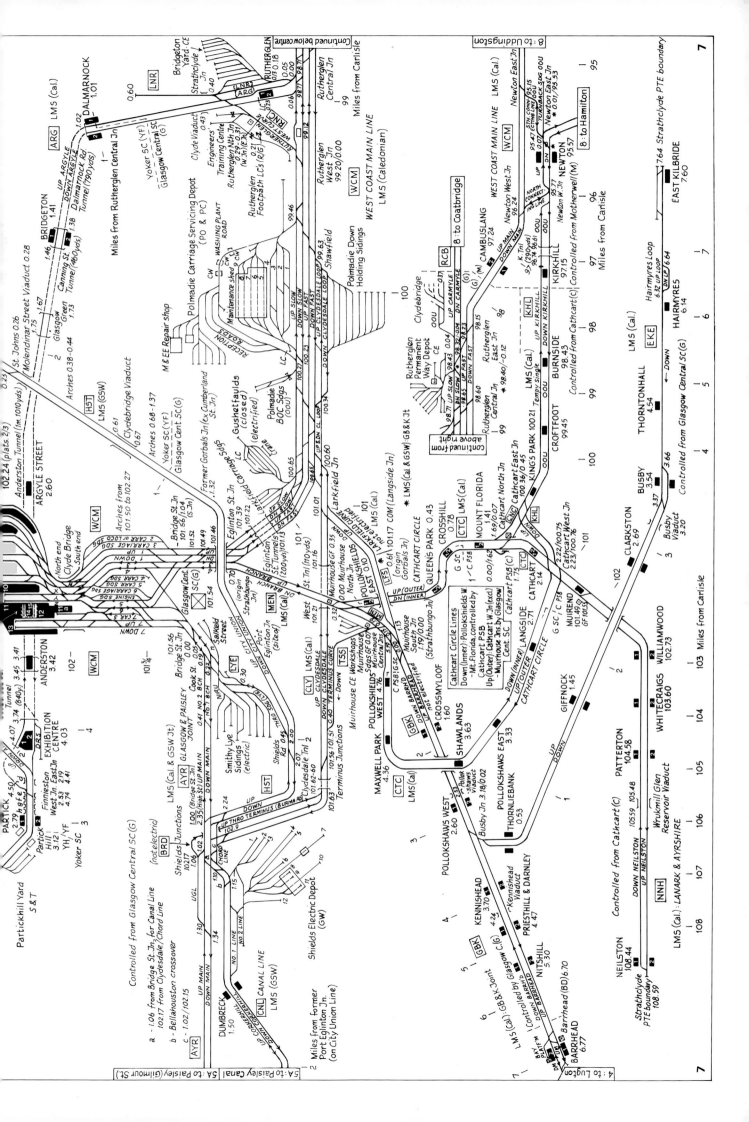

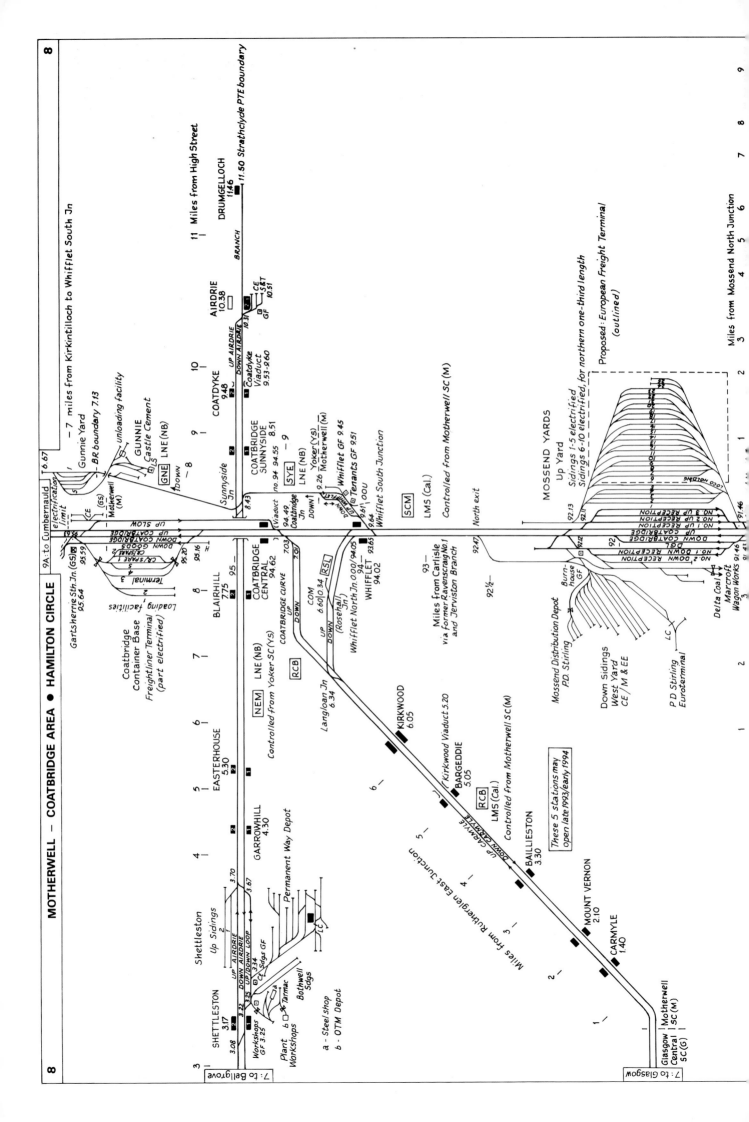

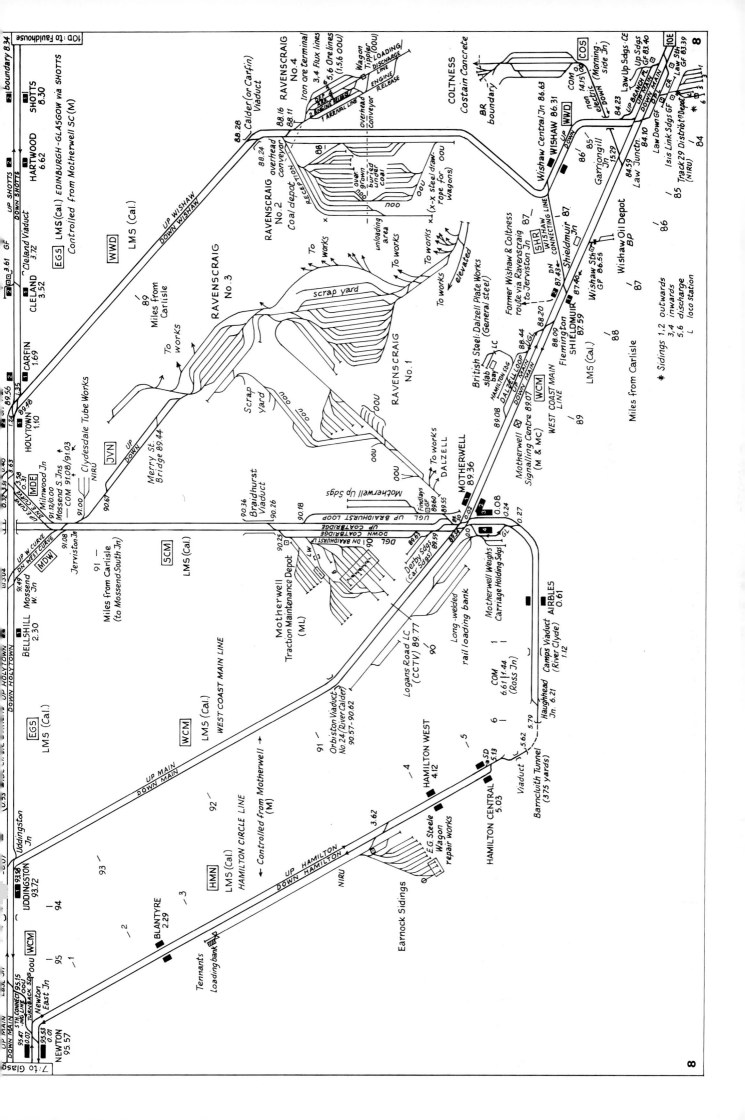

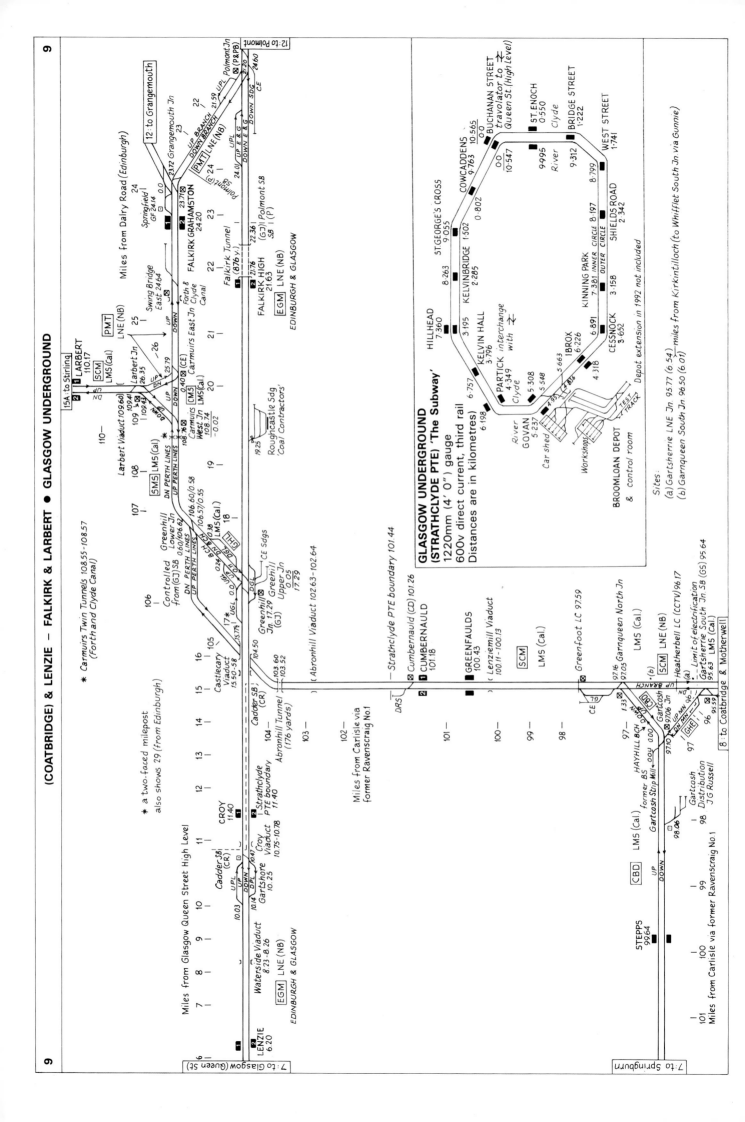

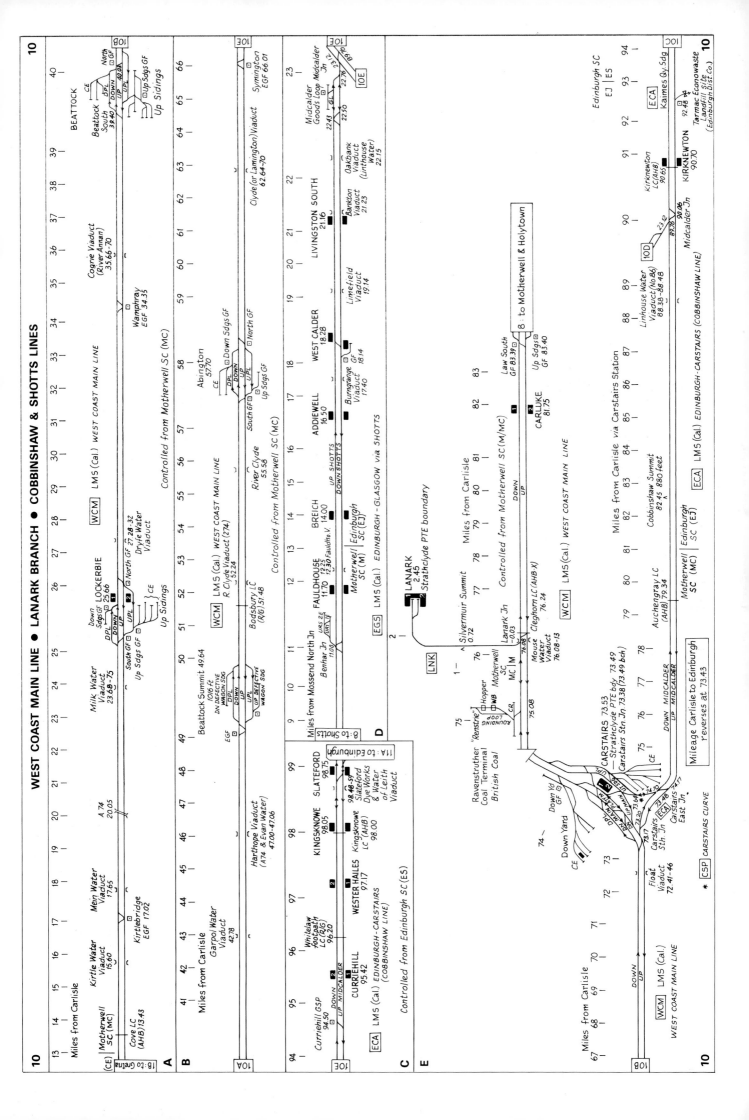

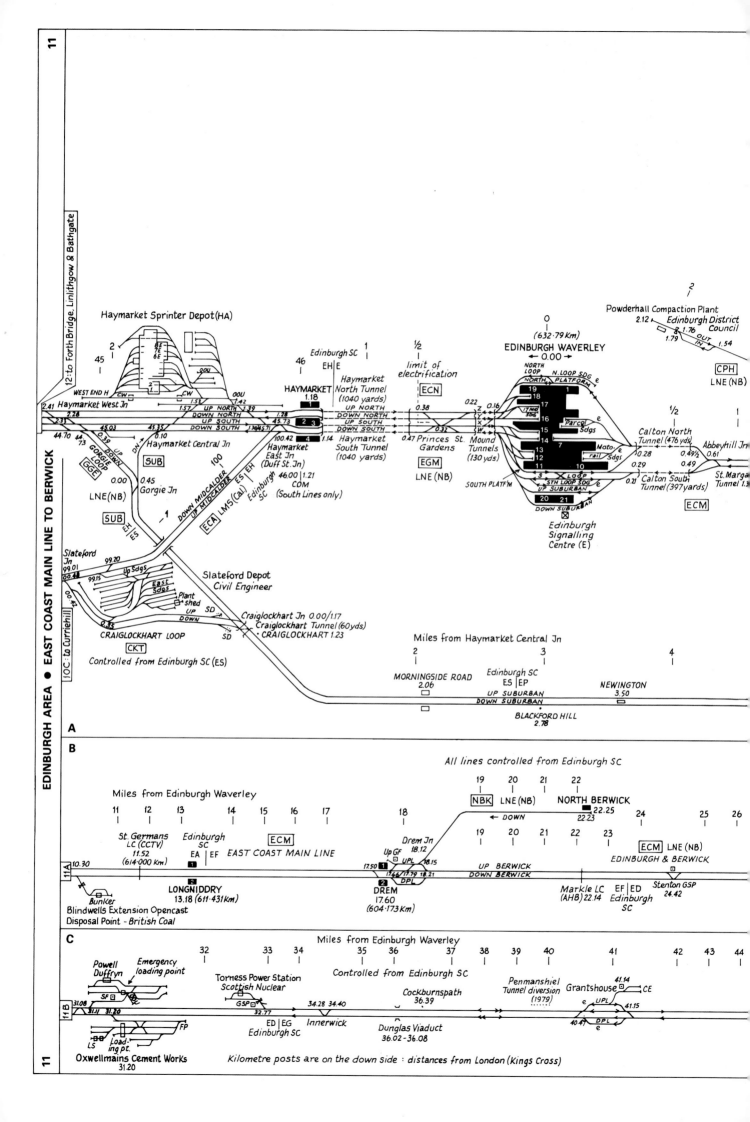

EDINBURGH AREA • EAST COAST MAIN LINE TO BERWICK

12: to Forth Bridge, Linlithgow & Bathgate

Haymarket Sprinter Depot (HA)

Powderhall Compaction Plant
2.12 Edinburgh District Council
1.79 IN 1.54 OUT
1.76

0
(632.79 Km)
EDINBURGH WAVERLEY
← 0.00 →

CPH
LNE (NB)

Edinburgh SC
EH | E

limit of electrification

½

Haymarket North Tunnel (1040 yards)

ECN

HAYMARKET 1.18

46

WEST END H
2.41 Haymarket West Jn
2.28
2.33
45.03
44.70 44.73
0.39

UP NORTH
DOWN NORTH
UP SOUTH
DOWN SOUTH

CW
1.53
1.57
1.42
1.39
1.28
45.35
45.71

UP NORTH
DOWN NORTH
UP SOUTH
DOWN SOUTH

100.42 | 1.14
4
Haymarket East Jn (Duff St. Jn)

0.38
0.22
0.16
Z
Y
X
W
0.32
0.47 Princes St. Gardens

EGM
LNE (NB)

Mound Tunnels (130 yds)

SOUTH PLATF'M

Calton North Tunnel (476 yds)
0.28 0.49½ 0.61 Abbeyhill
0.29 0.49 St. Marga...
Calton South Tunnel (397 yards) Tunnel 1.3...

NORTH LOOP
N. LOOP SDG e
NORTH PLATFORM
19 18 1
17
16 Parcel Sdgs
15
14 7
13 Moto-
12 rail
11 10 Sdgs
S X LOOP
STH LOOP SDG e
UP SUBURBAN
20 21
DOWN SUBURBAN

Edinburgh Signalling Centre (E)

ECM

SUB
Haymarket Central Jn
100
Haymarket SC

ECA LMS (Cal)
Edinburgh SC
46.00 | 1.21
COM (South Lines only)

SUB

Gorgie Jn
0.45
0.10

GORGIE LOOP
GGE
LNE (NB)
0.00

-1

Slateford Jn
99.01
00.44 99.15 99.20
Up Sdgs
EAST Sdgs

Slateford Depot
Civil Engineer

Plant shed SD
UP DOWN SD

Craiglockhart Jn 0.00/1.17
Craiglockhart Tunnel (60 yds)
CRAIGLOCKHART 1.23

0.35
CRAIGLOCKHART LOOP
CKT
Controlled from Edinburgh SC (ES)

10C : to Currichill

Miles from Haymarket Central Jn
2 3 4

MORNINGSIDE ROAD
2.06
Edinburgh SC
ES | EP
NEWINGTON
3.50

UP SUBURBAN
DOWN SUBURBAN

BLACKFORD HILL
2.78

A

B

All lines controlled from Edinburgh SC

Miles from Edinburgh Waverley
11 12 13 14 15 16 17 18

19 20 21 22
NBK LNE (NB)
NORTH BERWICK
22.25
← DOWN
22.23

19 20 21 22 23

St. Germans
LC (CCTV)
11.52
(614.000 Km)

Edinburgh SC
EA | EF

ECM
EAST COAST MAIN LINE

Drem Jn
18.12
Up GF
UPL
17.50 18.15
17.66/17.79 18.21
DPL

ECM LNE (NB)
EDINBURGH & BERWICK

UP BERWICK
DOWN BERWICK

Markle LC
(AHB) 22.14
EF | ED
Edinburgh SC
Stenton GSP
24.42

10.30
11A

Bunker
Blindwells Extension Opencast
Disposal Point - British Coal

LONGNIDDRY
13.18 (611.431km)

DREM
17.60
(604.173 Km)

C

Miles from Edinburgh Waverley
32 33 34 35 36 37 38 39 40 41 42 43 44

Powell Duffryn
Emergency loading point

Torness Power Station
Scottish Nuclear

Controlled from Edinburgh SC

Penmanshiel Tunnel diversion (1979)

Grantshouse
41.14
CE
UPL
41.15

SF
GSP
34.28 34.40
32.77

Cockburnspath
36.39

e

40.47
DPL
e

31.08
11B
31.11 31.20

ED | EG
Edinburgh SC
Innerwick

Dunglas Viaduct
36.02 - 36.08

FP
LS
Load-ing pt.
Oxwellmains Cement Works
31.20

Kilometre posts are on the down side : distances from London (Kings Cross)

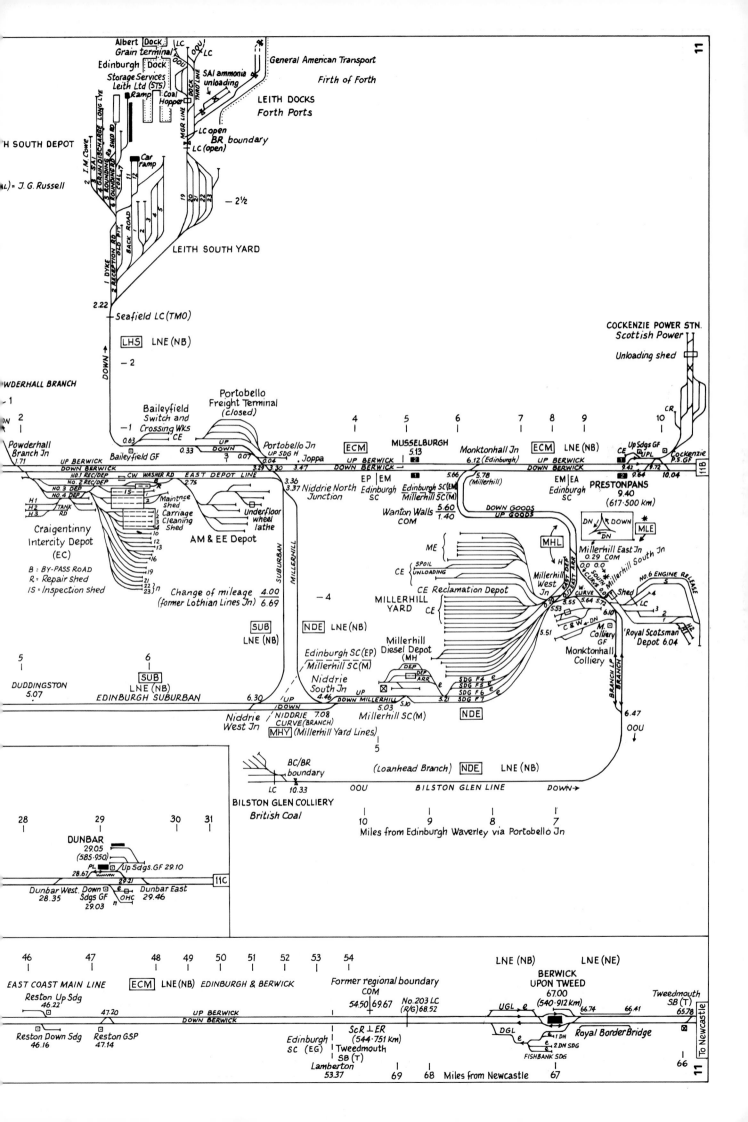

GRANGEMOUTH – POLMONT – INVERKEITHING – (EDINBURGH) ● BO'NESS & KINNEIL RAILWAY ● BATHGATE BRANCH ● BO'NESS & KINNEIL RAILWAY

13 to Dunfermline   13 to Burntisland

Inverkeithing Central Jn 13.21
Inverkeithing South Jn 13.05/00B *
Inverkeithing Car Park Footpath
LC (R/G) 0.05

INVERKEITHING 13.12
13 — 12.72
Inverkeithing Tunnel (418 yards)
12.53

Naval Base North GF 0.53 *
Limpetness Loop
J A White, scrapyard (NIRU)
& Sea Metals Ltd
Naval Base South GF 0.73 *
* controlled from Edinburgh

North Queensferry Tunnel (460 yards)
NORTH QUEENSFERRY 11.22
11.12

Forth Railway Bridge (2766 yards)
(1 mile 1006 yds)
9.47

DALMENY for South Queensferry 9.35
Forth Bridge Workshops
Dalmeny Up Sdgs GF 9.21
39.03/9.02 Dalmeny Jn

11.50
11.29
North Queensferry

ROSYTH ROYAL DOCKYARD
Babcock Thorn

Jamestown Viaduct
Ferry Toll Tunnel (130 yds)
MOD bdy 12 1.06 *
1.69
2.21

LNE (NB)
RHD
DOWN 2
UP FIFE
DN FIFE

ECN
EV | EY
11.16

Dalmeny Down Sdg GF 9.26
39
39.01
UPL
9 —
8 —
7 —
6 —

Edinburgh SC
EN | EH
EY | EH
ECN
LNE (NB)
EAST COAST LINE
11A to Edinburgh

SOUTH GYLE 4.45
DOWN FIFE
UP FIFE
45
3
44
3.28
43
2.41

(Almond Viaduct 7.22 – 7.26

EY | EH

42
41
40

UP E & G
DOWN E & G
EGM
LNE (NB)
EDINBURGH & GLASGOW

Newbridge Jn 3.52
38.63
38.59

Winchburgh Tunnel (352 yards)
Winchburgh Jn 34.54 34.57
EW | EN UP
EN | EW DOWN

DMY
LNE (NB)

Carriage shed
Bo'ness North Yard
3100 miles from High Street (Glasgow via Slamannan)

Wagon shed
Gds shed
East GF
BO'NESS 30.68
West GF
SB OOU
LS O
Wagon turntable
Loco workshop

BO'NESS & KINNEIL RAILWAY - Scottish Railway Preservation Society

KINNEIL HALT 29.63
Valve House
Lows Crossing
29.55 29.68
GF DOU GF

LNE (NB)
Miles from Glasgow Queen Street High Level

LINLITHGOW 29.56
UPL 30.18
Engineers Sdg 29.65

Avon Viaduct
28.06 – 26
Polmont | Edinburgh
SB (PB) SC (EL)

EGM
LNE (NB)
EDINBURGH & GLASGOW

New Oil Terminal - BP
Oil Terminal LC 3.67 3.70
Grangemouth Tongues LC 3.44
Exchange Siding
Macroft Engineering
Oil (gas) Terminal - BP
Depot Loop LC
BP Chemicals GF
ARR DEP
2.67

GRANGEMOUTH
Grangemouth Docks
Forth Ports
LC
3
BR/FP boundary 2.56
North GF 27.28
BIRKHILL 27.28
27.34
South GF 27.20
27.23 27.00

Avon Viaduct
Bo'ness GF 27.46
27.30 Bo'ness Jn
NIRU
Bo'ness 27.19

Manuel 26.18
25.78 26.05 26.10
DOWN MAIN
UP MAIN
27 – 27.05
27 – 27.00

Alcan (UK) Ltd
1.24 1.32
1.41

ORCHARDHALL BCH
OCL
— 2 miles from Swing Bridge Jn

Blue Circle Cement
Grangemouth West Yard
Grangemouth Traction Maintenance Depot (GM)
LMS (Cal)
Fouldubs Jn
TQT Haulage Depot (NIRU)
Q - TQT Haulage Depot (NIRU)
R - J Russell's Siding (NIRU)
2.12 1.51
2.46
NO 2 LOOP
UP/DN OIL TERMINAL
UP LOOP
DN LOOP
GMH

Grangemouth Jn
— 23 miles from Dalry Road (Edinburgh)

Polmont SB
Polmont Jn (P & PB)
POLMONT 24.73
2.60
P | PB
2.705
24.01 UPL
DPL
2.720
2.371
2.372
UP BRANCH
DOWN BRANCH

Marcroft Engineers
21.59
GMH
UPL
PMT
LNE (NB)
EGM
UP E & G
DOWN E & G
DOWN SDG
CE

9A to Falkirk Grahamston
9A to Falkirk High

Miles from High Street (Glasgow) via Airdrie
LIVINGSTON NORTH 29.03
Carmondean
Cawburn Jn 31.60
UPHALL 31.07
33
32
31
30
29
28
27
26

Birdsmill Viaducts road river
33.72-75 33.78-34.05
Ratho Viaduct (36 Arch Viaduct)
37.24 37.33 37.49
(7 Arch Viaduct)
38.01 38.19
COM
DP
36
37
35
34

35.32 35.48
EGM
LNE (NB)
Controlled from Edinburgh SC

BATHGATE 25.05
25.03 / 25
25.57
25.59
25.40
MAT
NBE
PASSENGER
FREIGHT
BATHGATE YARD 24.78
LNE (NB)
EDINBURGH & BATHGATE

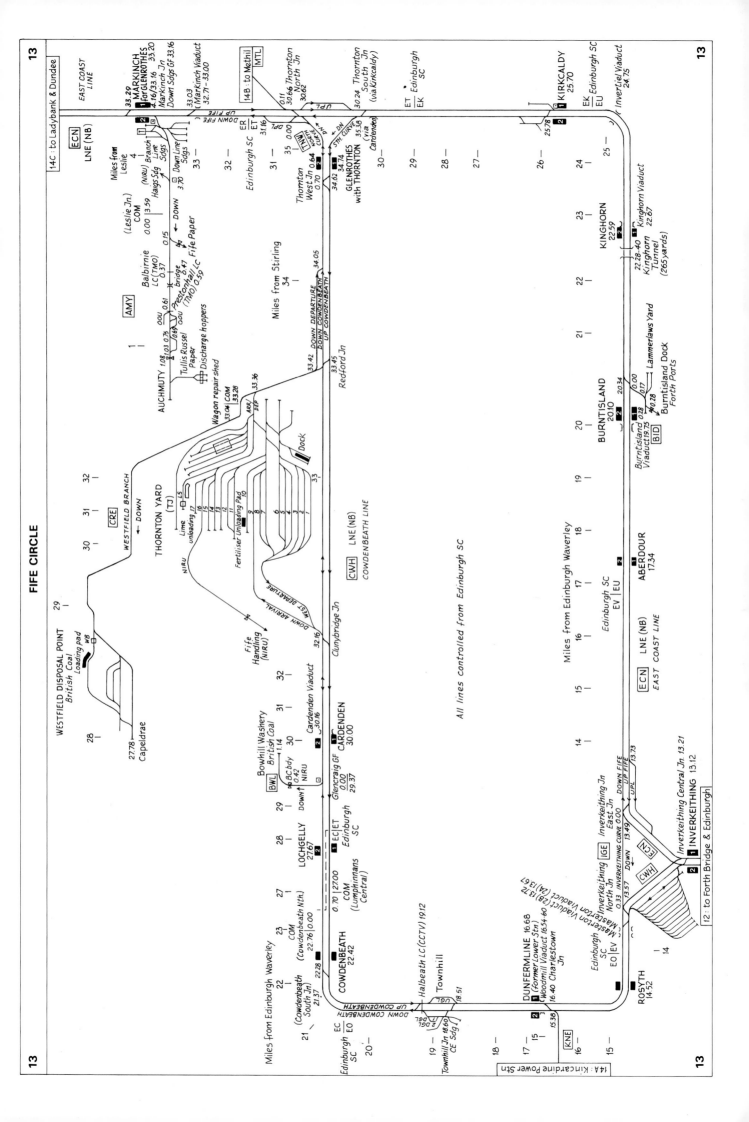

FIFE CIRCLE

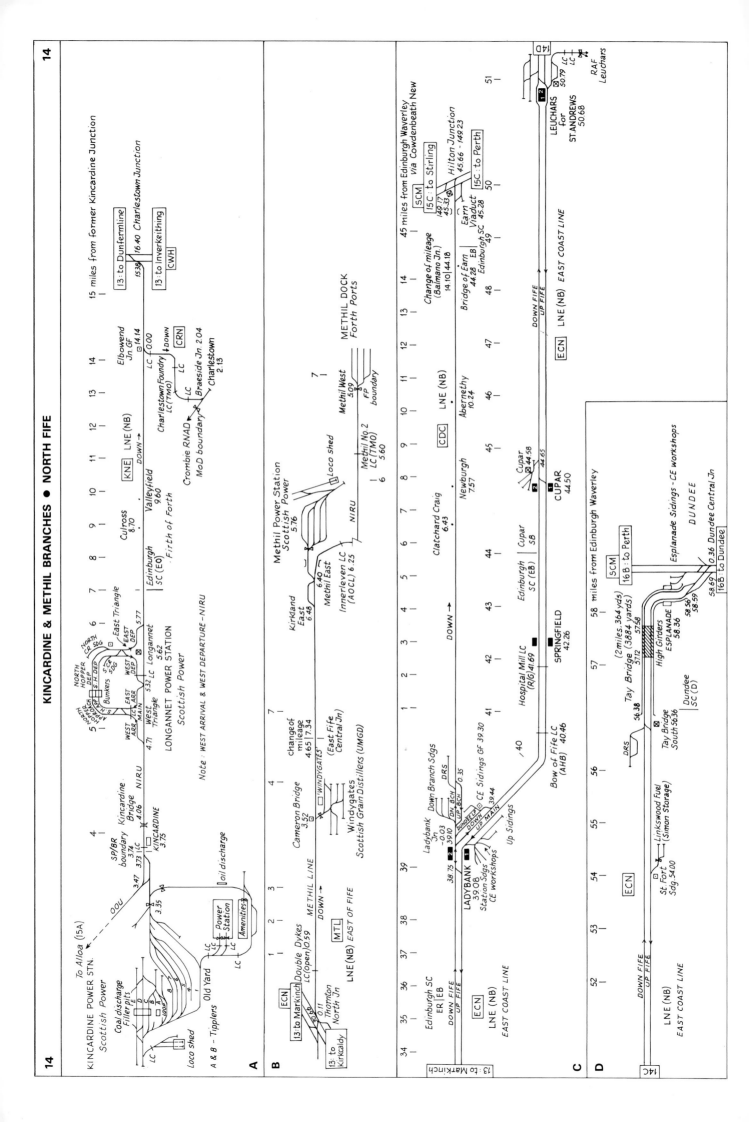

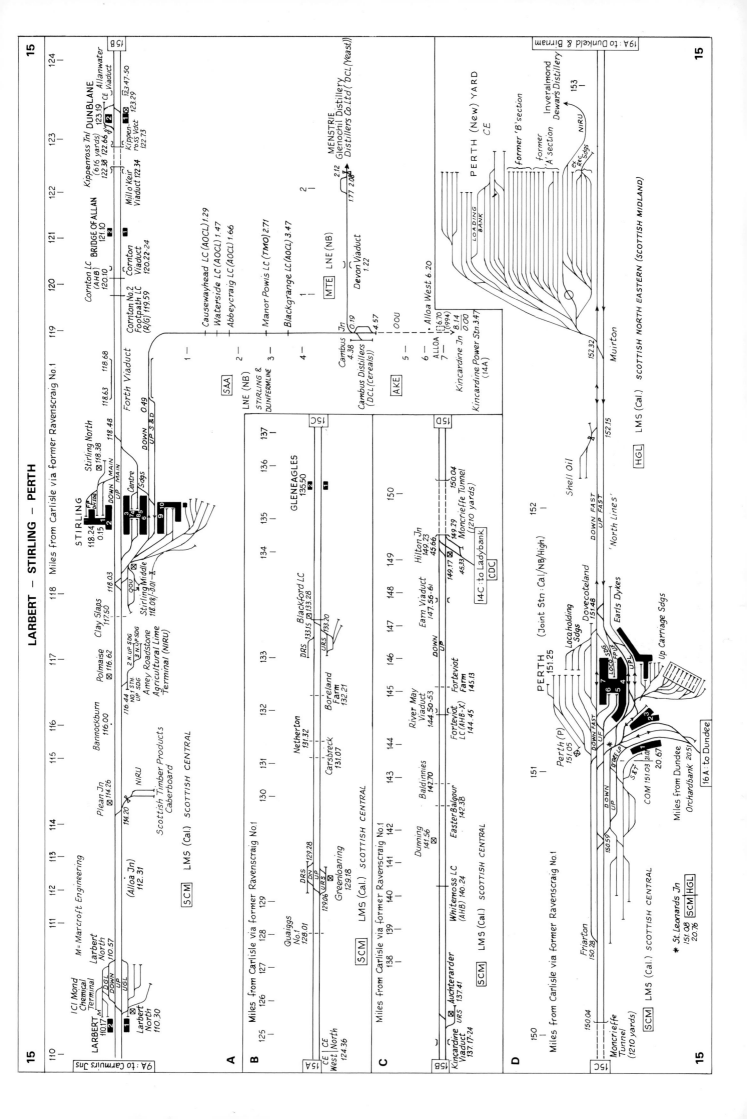

LARBERT - STIRLING - PERTH

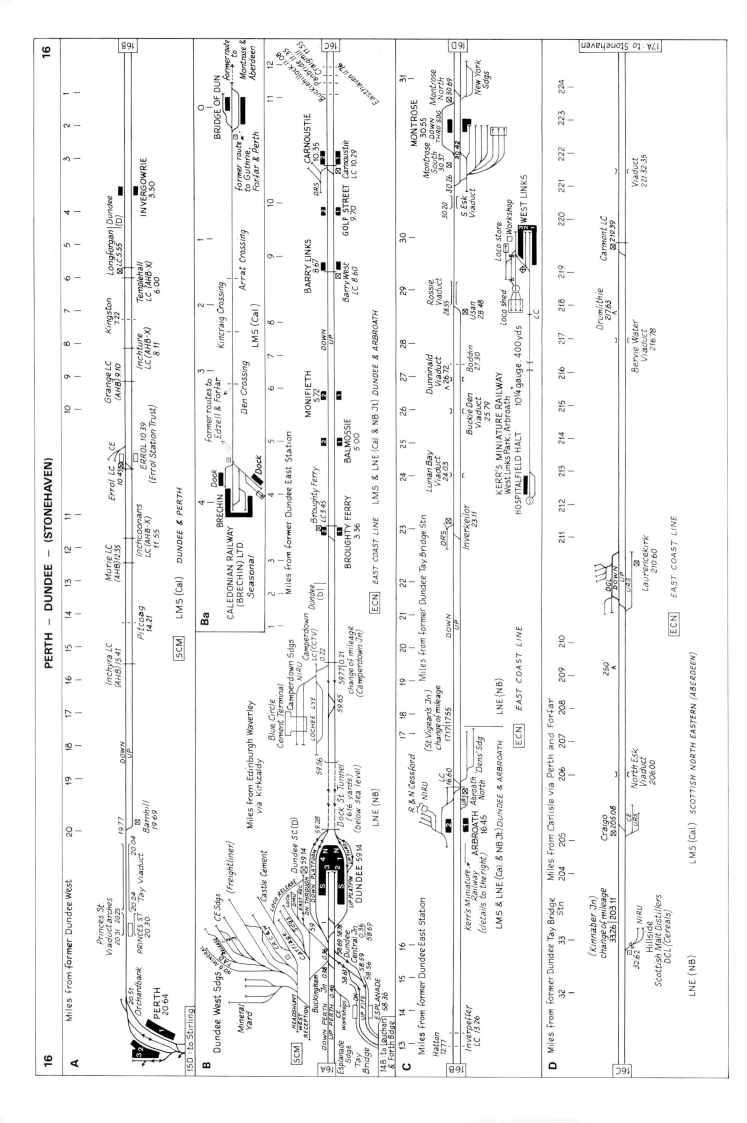

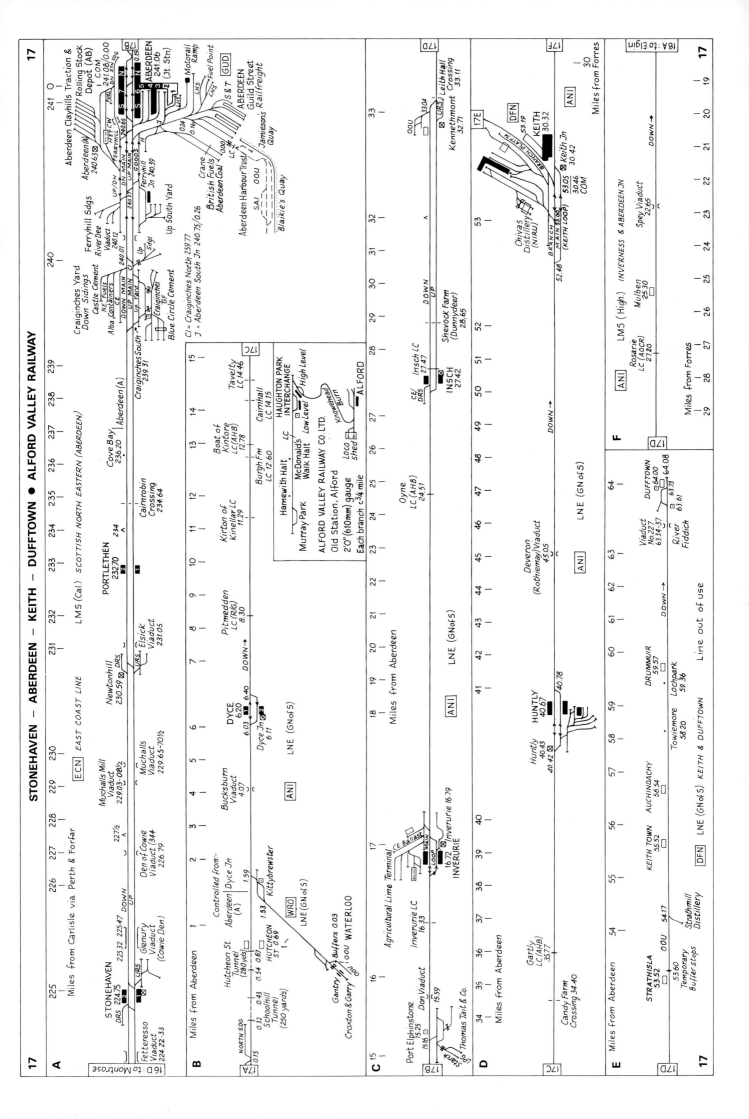

STONEHAVEN — ABERDEEN — KEITH — DUFFTOWN ● ALFORD VALLEY RAILWAY

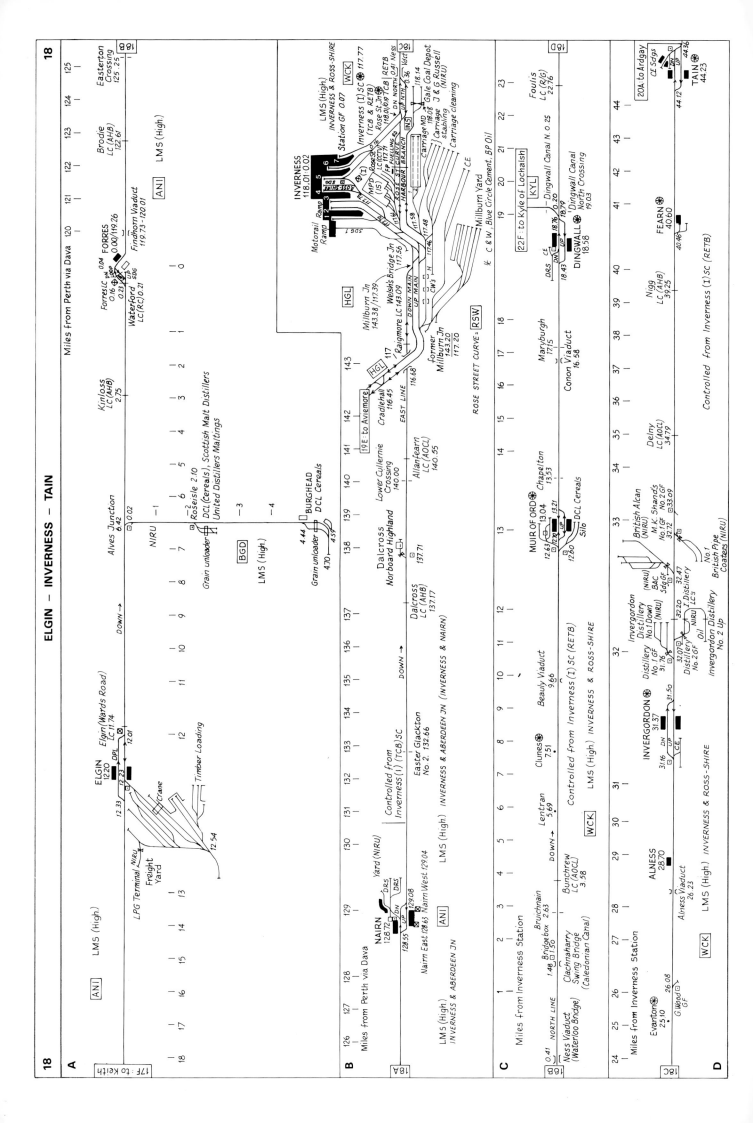

ELGIN — INVERNESS — TAIN

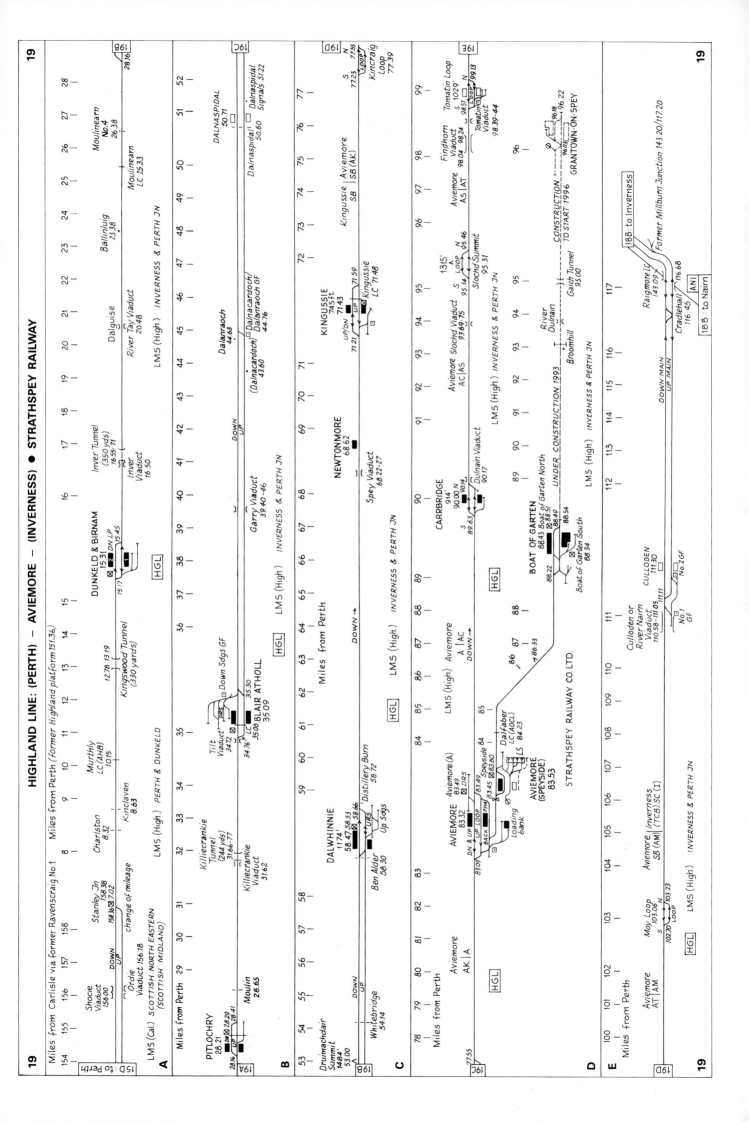

HIGHLAND LINE: (PERTH) – AVIEMORE – (INVERNESS) ● STRATHSPEY RAILWAY

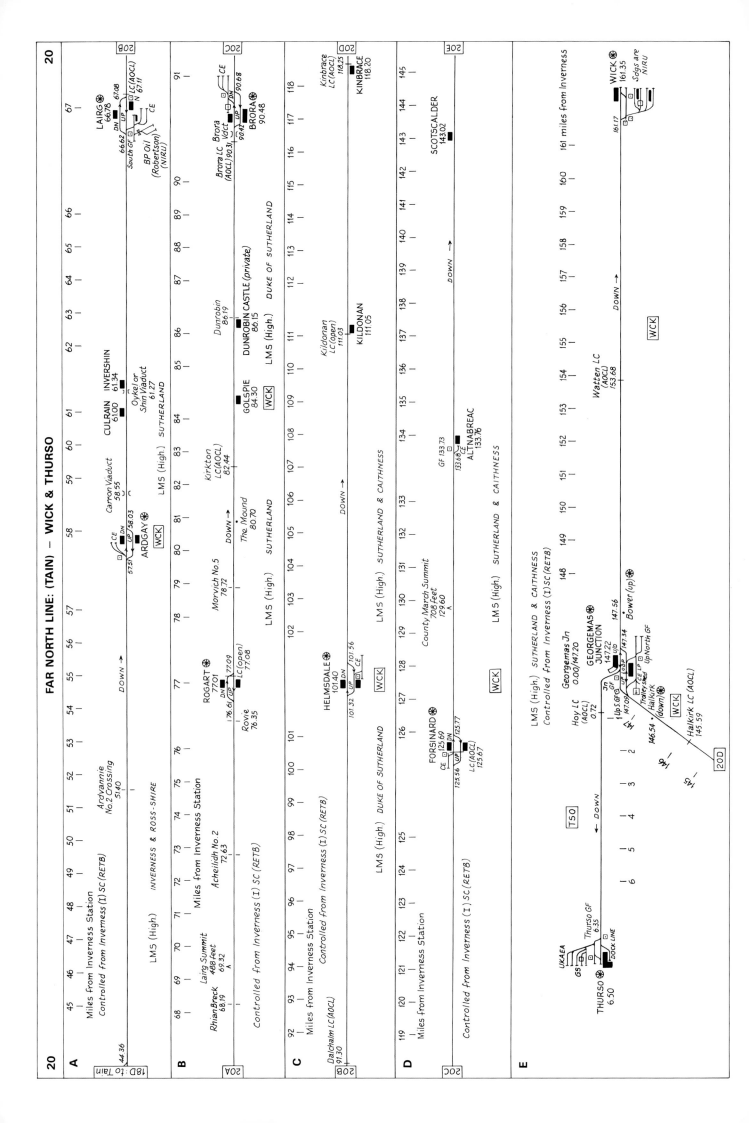

A

20B

LAIRG ✳ 66·78
DN 67·08
UP LC(AOCL) 67·11
N 6711
South GF 66·62
BP Oil (Robertson) (NIRU)
CE

Ardvannie No.2 Crossing 51·40

DOWN →

Miles from Inverness Station

Controlled from Inverness (I) SC (RETB)

LMS (High)   INVERNESS & ROSS-SHIRE

44·36
18D: to Tain

45 46 47 48 49 50 51 52 53 54 55 56 57 58 59 60 61 62 63 64 65 66 67

B

20C

Laing Summit 488 feet 69·32
RhianBreck 68·19
68·61
Achcilidh No.2 72·63

Miles from Inverness Station

ROGART ✳ 77·01
DN
UP 77·09
LC (open) 77·08
CE
Rovie 76·35

CE
Carron Viaduct 58·55
UP 58·03 DN
575t
ARDGAY ✳
WCK

CULRAIN 61·00   INVERSHIN 61·34
Oykel or Shin Viaduct 61·27

LMS (High)   SUTHERLAND

20A

Controlled from Inverness (I) SC (RETB)

68 69 70 71 72 73 74 75 76 77 78 79 80 81 82 83 84 85 86 87 88 89 90 91

C

20B

Dalchalm LC (AOCL) 91·30

Morvich No.5 78·72

The Mound 80·70

DOWN →

Kirkton LC(AOCL) 82·44

GOLSPIE 84·30
WCK

Dunrobin 86·19
DUNROBIN CASTLE (private) 86·15

LMS (High)   SUTHERLAND

Kildonan LC (open) 111·03
KILDONAN 111·05

Kinbrace LC(AoCL) 118·25
KINBRACE 118·20

DUKE OF SUTHERLAND

Miles from Inverness Station

Controlled from Inverness (I) SC (RETB)

92 93 94 95 96 97 98 99 100 101 102 103 104 105 106 107 108 109 110 111 112 113 114 115 116 117 118

D

20C

FORSINARD ✳
CE 125·69 DN
UP 125·77
125·56
LC (AOCL) 125·67

HELMSDALE ✳ 101·40
DN
UP 101·56
101·32 CE

WCK

County March Summit 708 feet 129·60
∧

DOWN →

ALTNABREAC 133·76
GF 133·73
133·68

SCOTSCALDER 143·02

Watten LC (AOCL) 153·68

DOWN →

20E

WCK

LMS (High)   SUTHERLAND & CAITHNESS

LMS (High)   SUTHERLAND & CAITHNESS

Miles from Inverness Station

Controlled from Inverness (I) SC (RETB)

119 120 121 122 123 124 125 126 127 128 129 130 131 132 133 134 135 136 137 138 139 140 141 142 143 144 145

E

THURSO ✳ 6·50
Thurso GF 6·35
UKAEA
G5
DOCK LINE

TSO

DOWN →

6
5
4
3
2
1

Hoy LC (AOCL) 0·72
Georgemas Jn 0·00/147·20
Jn 147·22
Up S GF UP 147·09
147·08 TCE LP
Trolley shed
LP LOD 147·34
Up North GF
Halkirk (down)
WCK
146·54
Halkirk LC (AOCL) 145·59

GEORGEMAS JUNCTION 147·56

Bower (up) ✳
147·56

Bower ✳

WCK

WICK ✳ 161·35
161·17
Sdgs are NIRU

161 miles from Inverness

146
145
20D

LMS (High)   SUTHERLAND & CAITHNESS
Controlled from Inverness (I) SC (RETB)

146 147 148 149 150 151 152 153 154 155 156 157 158 159 160 161

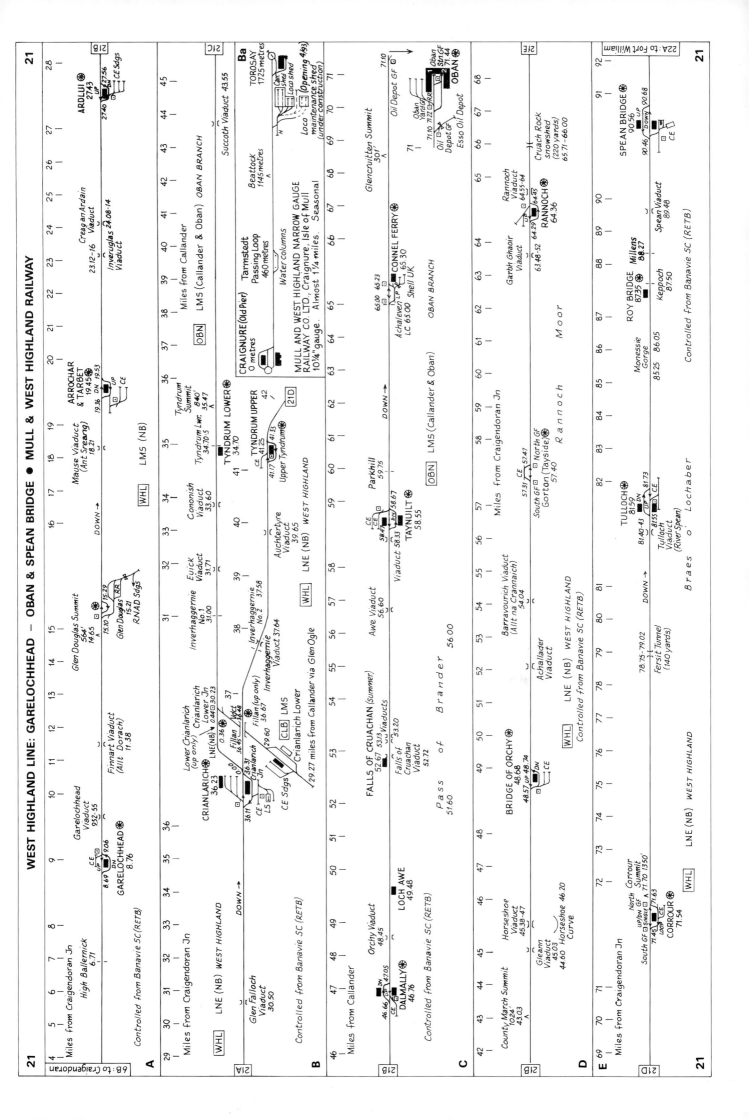

WEST HIGHLAND LINE: GARELOCHHEAD – OBAN & SPEAN BRIDGE ● MULL & WEST HIGHLAND RAILWAY

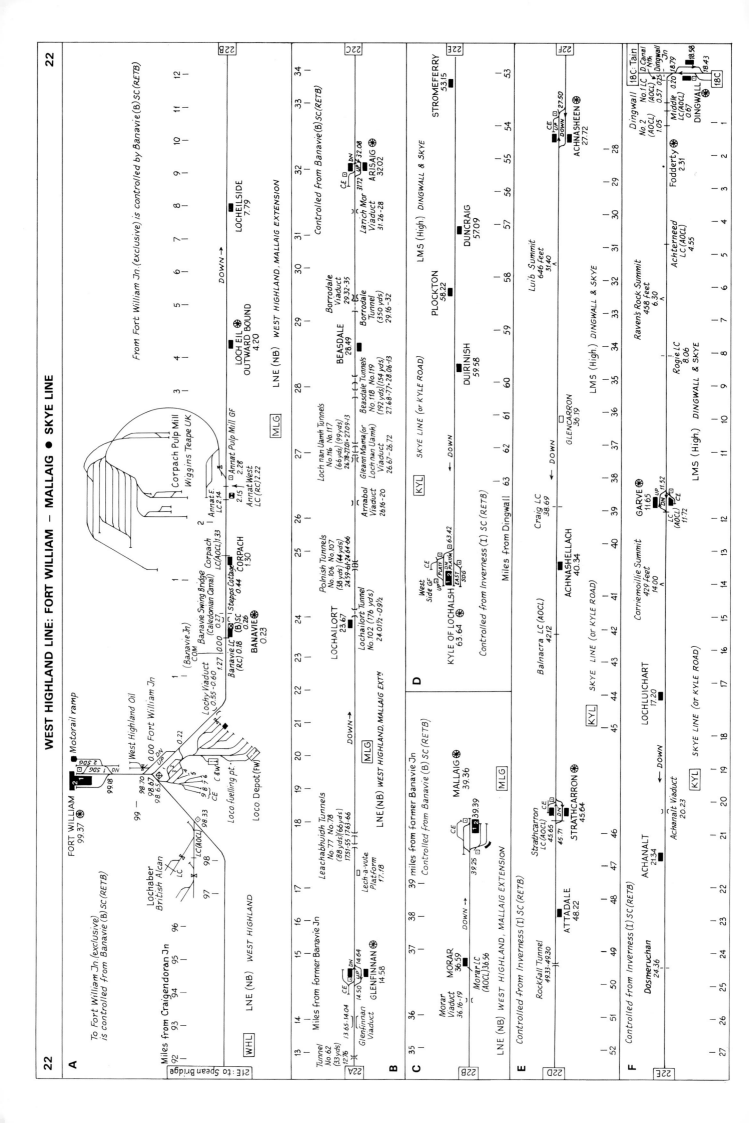

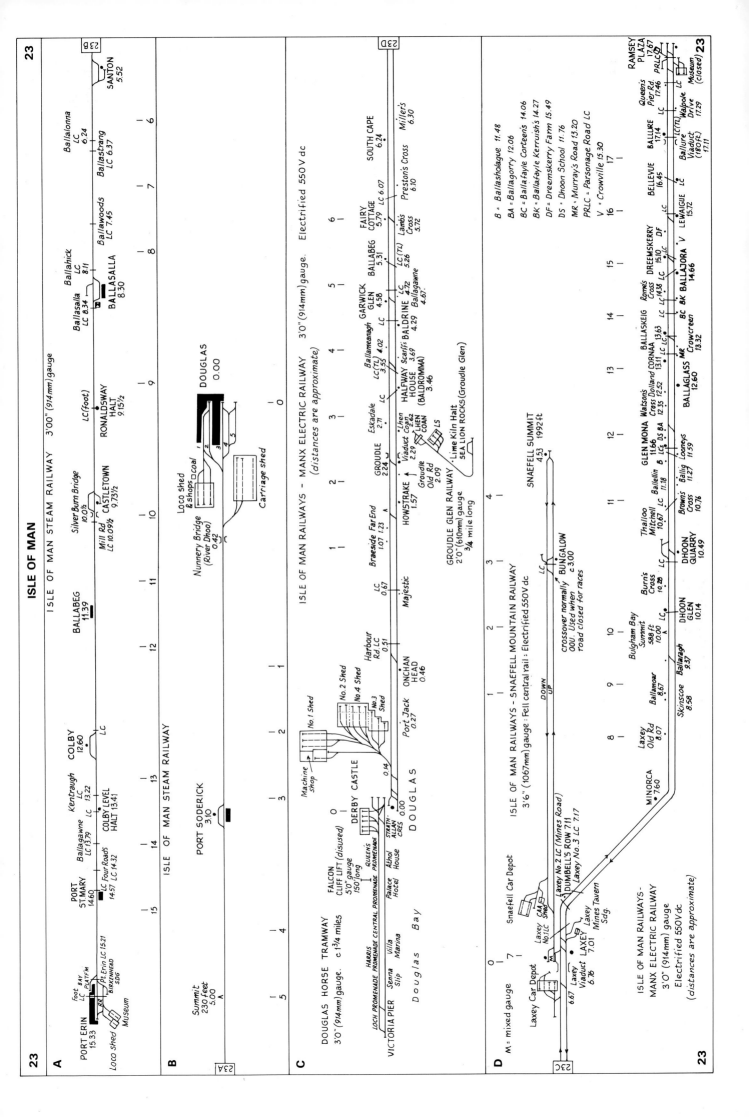

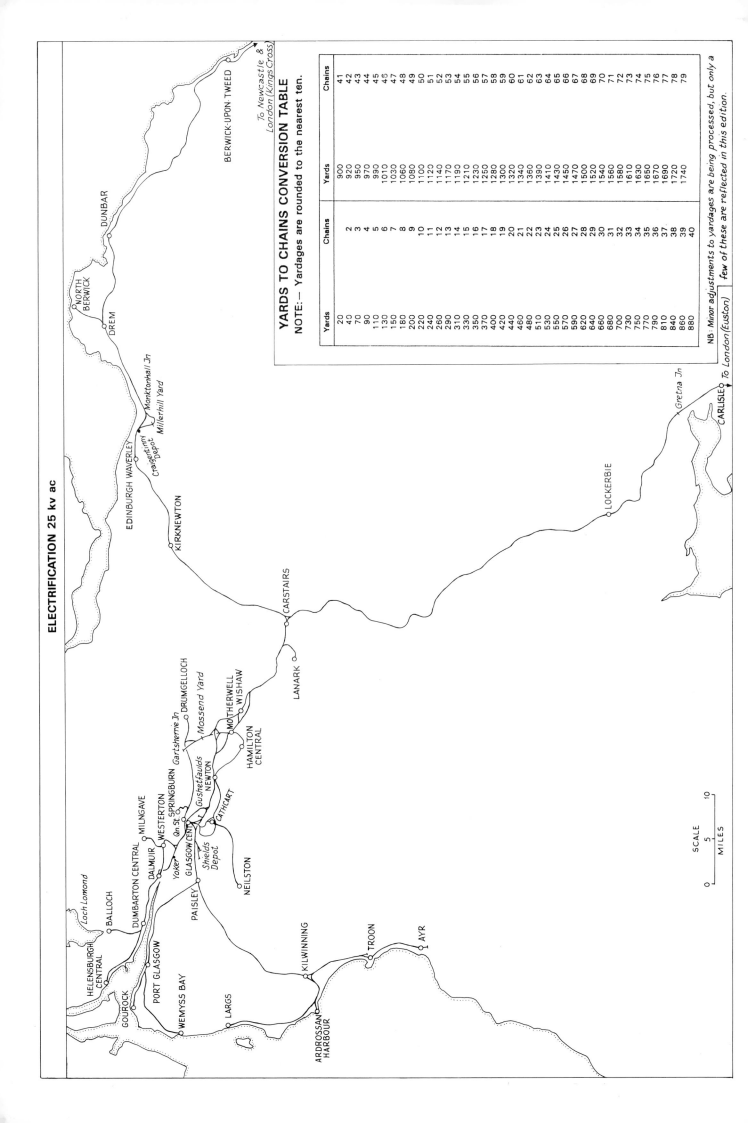

ELECTRIFICATION 25 kv ac

YARDS TO CHAINS CONVERSION TABLE

NOTE:— Yardages are rounded to the nearest ten.

Yards	Chains		Yards	Chains
20	1		900	41
40	2		920	42
70	3		950	43
90	4		970	44
110	5		990	45
130	6		1010	46
150	7		1030	47
180	8		1060	48
200	9		1080	49
220	10		1100	50
240	11		1120	51
260	12		1140	52
290	13		1170	53
310	14		1190	54
330	15		1210	55
350	16		1230	56
370	17		1250	57
400	18		1280	58
420	19		1300	59
440	20		1320	60
460	21		1340	61
480	22		1360	62
510	23		1390	63
530	24		1410	64
550	25		1430	65
570	26		1450	66
590	27		1470	67
620	28		1500	68
640	29		1520	69
660	30		1540	70
680	31		1560	71
700	32		1580	72
730	33		1610	73
750	34		1630	74
770	35		1650	75
790	36		1670	76
810	37		1690	77
840	38		1720	78
860	39		1740	79
880	40			

NB: Minor adjustments to yardages are being processed, but only a few of these are reflected in this edition.

SCALE

0   5   10

MILES

To Newcastle & London (Kings Cross)

To London (Euston)

HELENSBURGH CENTRAL — GOUROCK — PORT GLASGOW — WEMYSS BAY — BALLOCH — Loch Lomond — DUMBARTON CENTRAL — MILNGAVE — WESTERTON — DALMUIR — Yoker — SPRINGBURN — Qn. St. — GLASGOW CENTRAL — Shields Depot — PAISLEY — LARGS — NEILSTON — CATHCART — Gushetfaulds — NEWTON — HAMILTON CENTRAL — Gartsherrie Jn — DRUMGELLOCH — Mossend Yard — MOTHERWELL — WISHAW — LANARK — CARSTAIRS — KIRKNEWTON — EDINBURGH WAVERLEY — Craigentinny Depot — Monktonhall Jn — Millerhill Yard — DREM — NORTH BERWICK — DUNBAR — BERWICK-UPON-TWEED — LOCKERBIE — Gretna Jn — CARLISLE — ARDROSSAN HARBOUR — KILWINNING — TROON — AYR